DAVID ROSENMANN-TAUB

Poems and Commentaries

VOLUME I

David Rosenmann-Taub

Poems and Commentaries

an Anthology of Poems with a New Translational Strategy by

Kenneth Gorfkle

VOLUME I
REVISED EDITION

Copyright © 2022
All rights reserved for this edition copyright © 2022 Editorial A Contracorriente

Complete Library of Congress Cataloging-in-Publication Data
for the First Edition available at: https://lccn.loc.gov/2019939039

ISBN: 978-1-4696-7082-9 (paperback)
ISBN: 978-1-4696-7083-6 (ebook)

This is a publication of the Department of Foreign Languages and
Literatures at North Carolina State University. For more information visit
http://go.ncsu.edu/editorialacc.

Distributed by the University of North Carolina Press
www.uncpress.org

To Greg

TABLE OF CONTENTS

Introduction 1

Bibliography of David Rosenmann-Taub 9

CHAPTER 1. LIFE AND DEATH 13
PRELUDIO 14
LA CITA 18
De camarada a camarada, cuerpo, 22
Arambeles: 26
Entretanto el pasado, hacia la nada 30
¿Posteridad? 34
Con su soga oportuna me ahorca 38

CHAPTER 2. KNOWLEDGE AND SELF-KNOWLEDGE 43
"Florecí", brilla el pájaro. 44
ACADEMIA 48
Singular cuchitril: 52
ADMISERICÓRDIAM 56
SABIDURÍA 60
Derroté mis efigies: 64
"Con mutabilidad 68
Volubles alternativas 72

CHAPTER 3. GOD AND NATURE 77
No el cadáver de Dios lo que medito, 78
Varias malezas: 82
TAJRIJIM 86
Cuando, de vez en noche, soy real, 90
DEPEAPÁ 94

CHAPTER 4. DEVELOPMENT AND REGRESSION 99
NATURALEZA MUERTA 100
Ricos 104
...e interrogar a Dios, al techo, al adoquín, 108
Mi calavera, huérfana, 112
LA PRESTÍSIMA 116
MANANTIAL 120
YEMA 124

CHAPTER 5. EROTICISM 129
Gesto, dique, tarugo, 130
MADRIGAL 134
CONTRAESPEJOS 138
En las lavas sensuales busco siempre el regreso 142
Me imito: 146

CHAPTER 6. FAMILY, FRIENDS AND OTHERS 151
Tu estricto cúmulo 152
¡Vastedad de lo 156
La genilla de tu mampara 160
OLIGOPSONIO 164
¡Ir, sin reclamos, 168

CHAPTER 7. CONSCIOUSNESS AND UNCONSCIOUSNESS 173
FÍSICO 174
EREMITA 178
Cenit, imploras nadir. 182
Vértigo: 186
Endriago encabritado: 190
Por un resquicio exiguo 194
En el náufrago día de mi nave más bella 198

Introduction

David Rosenmann-Taub: biographical information.

BORN IN SANTIAGO, CHILE in 1927, the son of Jewish émigrés from Poland, David Rosenmann-Taub demonstrated prodigious talents from an early age. His mother, a consummate pianist, began teaching him piano when David was two years old. By the age of eight he had attained so much technical proficiency in the service of expression and creativity that he began to accept students. At the age of three, he began to dictate poems to his parents. At the age of five he adopted poetry, music and drawing as *his* vocations. During his childhood and adolescence, he wrote poems daily, while continuing his study of piano, composition and musical methodology. During his formative years Rosenmann-Taub also immersed himself in the natural sciences, linguistics and various languages.

Rosenmann-Taub published *El Adolescente* (The Adolescent), in 1945. In 1949, he published the first edition of the initial volume of *Cortejo y Epinicio* (Cortege and Epinicion), which won first prize in a city-wide poetry contest in 1952 sponsored by the Santiago Writers' Syndicate. His next book, *Los Surcos Inundados* (The Flooded Furrows) received the Premio Municipal de Poesía (The Municipal Prize of Poetry) in 1952. *El Regazo Luminoso* (The Shining Lap), which now forms a part of his recently published book *Jornadas* with the title of "Refugio," garnered the Premio Nacional de Poesía from the Universidad de Concepción (The National Prize of Poetry of the University of Concepción). By 1952, he was hailed as an "entirely new star" in the field of Chilean letters by Hernán Díaz Arrieta (Alone) and by Ricardo Latcham, the two leading literary critics of the country.

The poet continued to live and write in Chile over the course of the next twenty-three years, while supporting his family through teaching. Then, in 1975, after the death of his mother, the theft of many of his personal papers and the political situation in his country, he left Chile. He began a period of extensive travel, writing and lecturing throughout Latin America, the United States, and Europe. Between 1976 and 1978, he published another four books of poetry in Buenos Aires, Argentina. Nine years later, the poet settled in the United States, where he has lived ever since. He has not only continued his devotion to poetry but has also composed and recorded works for piano and other instruments; in addition he has dedicated himself to the plastic arts as well. Prolific in these domains, he has recorded over one hundred CDs of music and produced over one thousand drawings. Nevertheless, poetry remains his primary field; since 2002 he has published another nineteen books of poetry, including the republishing of some of his earlier works. Rosenmann-Taub's publications now span a full seven decades, and at this point in his life the poet is more active than ever, having published five new books in the last six years.

Throughout the course of his life, poets, critics, newspaper reviewers, editors, and journalists have consistently praised Rosenmann-Taub's poetry as work of the highest order. His poems have been translated and anthologized on four continents, set to music and dance, and performed on stage. Scholars worldwide have written academic articles and doctoral dissertations and held conferences and seminars on his poetry. His books are included in two of the most important repositories of Spanish literature worldwide: the University of Chile literary database and the Cervantes Virtual literary database.

Rosenman-Taub's poetics and thematic concerns

David Rosenmann-Taub wishes to understand and express the world and the human condition with rigor and exactitude. In a 2005 interview with Laura Castellanos in the Santiago de Chile newspaper *El Mercurio*, he states:

> ...to say the truth with precision, with certainty, as in a scientific investigation that has reached its ultimate consequences: that is a challenge. To accept this challenge is the real challenge. I don't see a difference between science and poetry. The function of art is to express knowledge in the most exact way possible; otherwise, it has neither function nor destiny. I came to the world to learn. If

I don't learn, I am less than nothing: I murder my time. It's already a lot to know a truth, almost a utopia and, sometimes, a complete utopia. To express it constitutes the domain of true poetry.[1]

Rosenmann-Taub expresses the nature of the world and the human condition. His linguistic and artistic knowledge permit him to express truths in his poetry. Due to its precision, his language is at times difficult.

In the same interview with Laura Castellanos, the poet declares, "Everything is for the sake of meaning. Poetry, when it is poetry, expresses knowledge in the most essential form."[2]

In another interview with Virginia Sarmiento, the poet states, "Sound, rhythm and silence, at the service of content, are fundamental; the contrary is text, but not poetry. To express, with beauty, horror or happiness is art: music, painting, sculpture, poetry. That was already evident to me when I was three years old."[3]

Some of the many themes that Rosenmann-Taub explores in his poetry include: the consciousness or lack of consciousness in mankind, the nature of God, the universe, and various immutable aspects of the human condition, such as love and friendship, the experience of the erotic, internal psychological conflicts, the alter ego, and the search for knowledge. Many of the poems included in this anthology address the aspect of the individual in relation to his or her own development.

Hermeneutics of the poetry of David Rosenmann-Taub

I have adopted Paul Ricoeur's model of hermeneutics as the basic method for the understanding and expression of these dense and complex poems. I argue that this is the same as a translation, since the goal of the hermeneut is the same as that of a translator: to understand and communicate the meaning of a text as faithfully as possible.[4] Ricoeur starts with the premise that the text is comprehensible, and begins his interpretation/translation process with "explanation:" a naïve interpretation that responds to the question "What does the text say?" He then proceeds to a more profound interpretation, one that responds to the question "What does the text talk about?" He concludes with the concept of appropriation, in which the reader absorbs this new understanding of the text and its world and, in the process, gains understanding and self-understanding.

For Ricoeur, the initial explanation of a text requires an exploration of its internal nature, without regard to its context, author, or audience. In this initial exploration of "what the text says," the text is understood as an object in itself: no external or subjective factors are considered. Accordingly, it is necessary to examine the meanings of the words on the page. Since Rosenmann-Taub often conveys multiple meanings using the same word, one must consider all of the words' meanings rather than attempting to choose the one meaning that might initially seem most appropriate.

Before leaving this first phase in the Ricoeurian hermeneutic process, the interpreter of Rosenmann-Taub's poems must further examine "what the text says." In his interviews as well as in commentaries to his own poems, the poet has insisted that the poem's form contributes to the understanding of its substance; and he himself has shown the ways in which he accomplishes this. Rhymes, alliteration, stanza configurations, and oddities or similarities in line length, rhythm, and meter may emphasize certain words or phrases within the poem. The poet's use of words within words produces additional meanings. Syntax and grammar can also highlight key words or ideas. Perhaps most important, the poems' highly figurative language enables the poet to set forth his multiple and complex ideas with brevity. Accordingly, to understand "what the text says," I explore these prosodic, syntactic, and rhetorical devices in addition to the words themselves.

The second phase of Ricoeurian hermeneutics requires a profound interpretation: verifying "what the text talks about." This requires a number of different strategies. According to Ricoeur scholar David Kaplan, Ricoeur "offers three rules for validating guesses of the meaning of the text."[5]

Starting with guesses, the translator employs the first rule of validation: the "rule of hermeneutic holism." Since poems are characterized by semantic unity, the underlying meaning of a symbol should always be related to the poem's global semantic sense. Once words and symbols are understood through their connection to that meaning, they can then inform us about other parts of the text. To translate the poems, I move back and forth between the various parts of the text, recognizing that all of the poem's parts are related to the text's global meaning and, accordingly, to each other.

The second rule of validation legitimizes the translator's subjective reaction to the text.[6] This reaction may be considered valid since subjectivity is an ontological given in the human condition. Ricoeur states that "A specific kind of one-sidedness is implied in the act of reading," thereby underscoring the point that subjectivity is the condition for the possibility of understanding.[7] Since the vast majority of Rosenmann-Taub's poems refer to universal themes, they speak collectively to all individuals: everyone is born, interacts with other people, journeys through life with varying degrees of consciousness, and confronts death. However, as they do so, the poems also speak to each individual as well, and Ricoeurian hermeneutics allows the incorporation of that subjective understanding into the poem's meaning without discounting its value.

The third rule of validation takes into account the fact that multiple meanings exist in any given text, and states that "...validation is not verification but an argumentative practice....".[8] I research the psychosocial characteristics of the author, his historical and cultural context, and all other available external information. I then examine various interpretations, using a "logic of subjective probability" to choose the best alternative. In this phase of understanding, I have the liberty to consider factors outside the text, in order to make it relevant to the reader. I use information gleaned from as many sources as possible to validate my interpretation. The location of the poem in the chapter and book where it appears, the poet's comments in interviews concerning his poetry and/or his own views of life; the poet's written commentaries on other poems; other previously understood poems, and even other analyses of Rosenmann-Taub's poetry may all shed light on the poem. The resulting translation thus achieves the "grounded subjectivity" which is at the core of Ricoeurian hermeneutics.[9] As my world fuses with that of the author's, I achieve a new understanding of the text.

Appropriation and transformation constitute the last stage of the Ricoeurian hermeneutic model. Initially distanced from the text, I have now "appropriated" it and become transformed. The poem has presented me with a new way of thinking about the world, or about myself. When I understand what the poem says and incorporate and synthesize it with my own perspective, I change.

Translating the poetry of David Rosenmann-Taub

For translation scholars, the test of an adequate translation is the measure of its fidelity to the original text: the translator's goal is to transmit the text's meaning while reproducing its form and function. However, to achieve this textual fidelity in poetry translation at times seems impossible, and

Rosenmann-Taub's poetry is no exception in this aspect. Since language is tied to cultural context, words in one language may not exist in another. The poet's polysemic language precludes exact translation, and his abbreviated metaphors may require entire paragraphs to adequately express their meaning. Furthermore, the sound, rhythm, and meter of his poems do not carry over from one language to another. As a result, the traditional form of translation, where the translator preserves the form of the original poem through employing word-for-word semantic equivalents rarely conveys the full meaning of his poems.

In order to elucidate the full richness of these poetic texts, I adopt a recently developing translation theory called translational hermeneutics: the translator does not translate the text itself, but instead first seeks to deeply understand it, and then communicates his or her mental construct of the text. This communication may be considered a translation even though it may have no formal relationship to the original text, since expressive liberty results in a text that is more faithful to the substance of the original text. This new translational theory, which has the capacity to include all the elements of the text, enables me to accurately communicate my understanding of the text.

In this study of the poems of Rosenmann-Taub, I search for meaning as much in the form of the poem as in its content, in order to finally express this understanding with a paraphrase. The paraphrase is the most faithful expression of the author's intention, insofar as 1) it can freely express my understanding of the text without being chained to its words; and 2) it attends to the complexity of sense as it is transmitted not just from one language to another, but from one time, place, and culture to another as well.[10] The goal is to capture the greatest part of the information crystalized in the poem. This translational strategy has the greatest possibility of representing the meaning of the text.

Notes on the translations

I first present the poems in their original Spanish, followed by a traditional translation. I then paraphrase the poem to amplify and clarify its content to the maximum extent possible. These paraphrases range from a paragraph to a page in length. Like a traditional translation, the ideas expressed in the paraphrase correspond directly to the words of the poem, except that whereas a traditional translation employs only one word to express the meaning of its corresponding word, the paraphrase can employ a sentence or even a paragraph to unpack the meaning of that word. Occasionally I insert a prologue to orient the reader or, at times, an epilogue for further clarification.

To remain as faithful to the poem's substance as possible, I maintain the poem's mood, be it serious, sarcastic, light- or dark-humored, reflective, declarative, or confrontational. Since the poems are universal and, by virtue of that fact, personal in nature, I communicate the poem's contents more directly through speaking in my own voice. My translational model allows for subjectivity on the part of the translator, so at times I take the liberty of inserting my own words or complementary ideas to amplify the understanding of the text.

Rosenmann-Taub's poems cover a wide variety of concerns. My goal is to give a taste of the poet's thought in a number of different domains. I do not presume that my translations are definitive; with his or her own personal and literary background, the reader may find other interpretations. However, these translations allow a foot in the door, so to speak, and – for those who wish to continue with this challenging and profound poetry – a preliminary understanding of Rosenmann-Taub's poetic form and substance to assist them in their own investigations.

Notes

1. Castellanos, Laura. 2005. "'Vine al mundo a aprender.' Rosenmann-Taub." *Reforma* 5/2005, 1.
2. Castellanos, 2.
3. Interview of the poet with Virginia Sarmiento, July, 2010.
4. David Kaplan, *Ricoeur's Critical Theory*. Albany: State University of New York Press, 2003, 67.
5. Ricoeur notes that "like any object, a text can only be perceived from a particular perspective but never from all perspectives at once" (Kaplan, 68).
6. Kaplan, 68.
7. Ricoeur, Paul. *Interpretation Theory: Discourse and the Surplus of Meaning*, 78.
8. Stolze observes that "grounded understanding" of the text results when the translator places him or herself "within the relevant cognitive environment of knowledge; ...to approach...a text, right from the beginning as being embedded in a foreign cognitive environment" (69).
9. Machulskaya, Olga. 2015. "The problem of the adequacy of translation as conceptualized by Paul Ricoeur", *Noema* 6/2: 2.
10. This argument is neither new or unusual. See, for example, translator

and scholar S.O. Kolawole, who emphasizes that fidelity in translation refers to the sense and not the words of the text (2). Also, see Amparo Hurtado-Albir (1990:118), who defines fidelity in relation to three things: 1) the author's intention, 2) the target language, and 3) the reader. Finally, Radegundis Stolze, one of the principal founders of translational hermeneutics, has stated that "[t]he translator does not choose between options, but attempts to express the thought in the correct way in the target language, liberating himself from the grammatical source text (145)".

Works Cited

Castellanos, Laura. 2005. "'Vine al mundo a aprender.' Rosenmann-Taub." Reforma 5/2005: 2.

Hurtado-Albir, Amparo. 1990. "La notion de fidélité en traduction". *Collection Traductology* 5.

Kaplan, David. *Ricoeur's Critical Theory*. Albany: State University of New York Press, 2003.

Machulskaya, Olga. 2015. "The problem of the adequacy of translation as conceptualized by Paul Ricoeur". *Noema* 6/2: 2.

Mantzavinos, C. 2009. "What Kind of Problem is the Hermeneutic Circle?". C. Mantzavinos (ed.), *Philosophy of the Social Sciences. Philosophical Theory and Scientific Practice*. Cambridge: Cambridge University Press, 299 - 11.

Ricoeur, Paul. *Interpretation Theory: Discourse and the Surplus of Meaning*. Fort Worth, Texas: Christian University Press, 1976.

Sarmiento, Virginia. Interview with David Rosenmann-Taub. July 2010.

Schleiermacher, Friedrich. *Hermeneutics and Criticism*. Cambridge: Cambridge University Press, 1998.

Stolze, Radegundis. *The Translator's Approach: An Introduction to Translational Hermeneutics with Examples from Practice*. Berlin: Frank & Timme, 2011.

Bibliography of
David Rosenmann-Taub

※

THE WORK OF DAVID Rosenmann-Taub spans seven decades. However, his publications fall into three distinct periods. The first period, from 1949 to 1952, proclaims the arrival of a new star in the Latin American poetic firmament: Rosenmann-Taub published his first four books, among which three are recognized with literary prizes and to critical acclaim. The second period, from 1976 to 1978, witnesses the publication of three new books and a second edition of his first published work, *Cortejo y Epinicio*. The poet's third and most prolific publishing period, beginning in 2002 and continuing through the present, marked by his alliance with LOM Ediciones and the Corda Foundation (a nonprofit organization that preserves and promotes his work), has resulted in another nineteen published works.

2020   *GLOSA*, Mandora Press, New York, New York.
2018   *Jornadas*, LOM Ediciones, Santiago, Chile.
2017   *Alm-ería*, Editorial Pre-textos, Valencia, España.
2016   *Trébol de Nueve*, LOM Ediciones, Santiago, Chile.
2015   *Oó, o*, Editorial Pre-textos, Valencia, España.
2014   *Los Surcos Inundados*, LOM Ediciones, Santiago, Chile.
2013   *La Noche Antes*, LOM Ediciones, Santiago, Chile Volume IV of the tetralogy *Cortejo y Epinicio*
2013   *Cortejo y Epinicio*: tetralogía, boxed set with the four volumes, LOM Ediciones, Santiago, Chile.
2013   *El Zócalo*, LOM Ediciones, Santiago, Chile First volume of the tetralogy, previously entitled *Cortejo y Epinicio*. Now published, in its fourth printing, with its definitive title.
2013   *En Un Lugar de la Sangre*, Mandora Press, Canada. Contains two CDs

	with the author reading the poems, and a DVD of two paintings.
2011	*La Opción*, LOM Ediciones, Santiago, Chile Volume III of the tetralogy *Cortejo y Epinicio*
2008	*Quince: Autocomentarios*, LOM Ediciones, Santiago, Chile Contains a CD with the author reading the poems.
2007	*Auge*, LOM Ediciones, Santiago, Chile.
2006	*Los Despojos del Sol: Anandas I y II*, second edition, LOM Ediciones, Santiago, Chile.
2005	*Poesiectomía*, LOM Ediciones, Santiago, Chile.
2004	*El Cielo en la Fuente / La Mañana Eterna*, second edition, LOM Ediciones, Santiago, Chile.
2004	*País Más Allá*, LOM Ediciones, Santiago, Chile.
2003	*El Mensajero*, LOM Ediciones, Santiago, Chile Volume II of the tetralogy *Cortejo y Epinicio*.
2002	*Cortejo y Epinicio*, third edition, LOM Ediciones, Santiago, Chile.
1983	*Al rey su trono*, inspired by the aphorisms of Nahúm Kamenetzky, Esteoeste, Buenos Aires, Argentina.
1978	*Los Despojos del Sol: Ananda Segunda*, Esteoeste, Buenos Aires, Argentina.
1978	*Cortejo y Epinicio*, second edition, Esteoeste, Buenos Aires, Argentina.
1977	*El Cielo en la Fuente*, Esteoeste, Buenos Aires, Argentina.
1976	*Los Despojos del Sol: Ananda Primera*, Esteoeste, Buenos Aires, Argentina.
1962	*Cuaderno de Poesía*, Taller Edición 99, Santiago, Chile.
1952	*La Enredadera del Júbilo*, Cruz del Sur, Santiago, Chile.
1951	*Los Surcos Inundados*, Cruz del Sur, Santiago, Chile.
1951	*El Regazo Luminoso*: included in *Jornadas* with the title "Refuge." Prize awarded from the University of Concepción.
1949	*Cortejo y Epinicio*, Cruz del Sur, Santiago, Chile First volume of its tetralogy.

CHAPTER 1

Life and Death

PRELUDIO

1. Life and Death

PRELUDIO

Después, después, el viento entre dos cimas
y el hermano alacrán que se encabrita,
y las mareas rojas sobre el día.
Voraz volcán: aureola sin imperio.
El buitre morirá: laxo castigo.
Después, después, el himno entre dos víboras.
Después, la noche que no conocemos
y, extendido en lo nunca, un solo cuerpo
callado como luz. Después, el viento.

(El Zócalo, p. 5)

PRELUDE

After, after, the wind between two peaks,
and the brother scorpion that rears up,
and the red tides over the day.
Voracious volcano: halo without empire.
The vulture will die: lax punishment.
After, after, the hymn between two vipers.
After, the night which we don't know
and, extended in the nevermore, one sole body
silent like light. After, the wind.

1. Life and Death

"PRELUDIO" is the first poem of the first book of the poet's tetralogy *Cortejo y Epinicio*. The poem hypothesizes death not only as the end of life, but also as its cause and companion. Images of death in life abound: the scorpion, the red tides, the volcano, the vulture, the vipers and the unknowable night that comes at one's demise.

After death, life. I: a wind, alive and mobile, channeled between the peak of the beginning and that of the end.

Enemies surround me. The scorpion: rearing up to block me from my goals. The red tides and the voracious volcano: Nature, wishing to cover me, drown me in my own blood, devour me. Although fearsome in appearance, Nature's substance is as ephemeral as mine: the scorpion perishes, the eruption ceases, the lava congeals, and death prevails over all. Even the vulture, the bird who feeds on death, will die: its punishment is weak, since this scavenger bird, who lives only to eat, is barely conscious.

The cycle continues: life always comes after death, always threatened by death. The hymn of consciousness: always a prey of the vipers of laziness and ignorance. After death, life: an unknowable night through which I blindly wander, groping for meaning. After life, death: my body, an extension in time and space, silent and luminous. After death, life: I, a wind, alive and mobile.

LA CITA

LA CITA

Preguntarán en casa
por mí. ¡Tanto feriado sin tu zarpa!
Sepelio, ¿no me amas?

Paulatino diluvio.
Neutralidad. Borneo hacia el estuco.
Dios, celoso: «¿Te aburro?»

(El Mensajero, p.12)

THE DATE

They will be asking at home
for me. Such a vacation without your claw!
Burial, don't you love me?

Gradual deluge.
Neutrality. I twist towards the stucco.
God, jealous: "Am I boring you?"

1. Life and Death

In each moment of life, the individual has a choice: life or death? The poem portrays the patterns of conventional and unconscious life which render it little different than physiological death. Yet the poet also points to the possibility of life that might exist after death.

Tired of life, I contemplate my future death. My family will ask for me; but already I will no longer be among the living. Finally, rest and relief, a vacation from your claw, Life! Flirting with Death: "Why not take me now? Perhaps you don't love me?"

My life: a slow deluge of unconsciousness that moment by moment engulfs me. My passive acceptance of the circumstances and exigencies of life may be seen as death in life. I continually twist towards life's superficial aspects and distance myself from its essential ones; it is as if I have an ever-present and simultaneous date with Death and Life, and constantly turn towards the former. In fact, my attraction to Death is so obvious that God, Creator of life and jealous of Death's power, asks me if He bores me.

De camarada a camarada, cuerpo,

1. Life and Death

De camarada a camarada, cuerpo,
te he pedido. Me has dado.
Pídeme. Anhelo darte
mi riqueza: los verbos del silencio:
sus hálitos
empiezan a habitarme.

(La Noche Antes, p.223)

As one comrade to another, body,
I have made demands of you. You have given to me.
Make demands of me. I yearn to give you
my richness: the words of silence:
their breaths
begin to inhabit me.

At the end of life consciousness speaks to the body, recognizing the importance of this intimate relationship:

"Body of mine, you are my friend and I am yours.
You have always given what I have asked.
Now on the threshold of death, I begin to be the home of silence.
I want you to inhabit me."

Arambeles:

1. Life and Death

Arambeles:
fanales: secos ríos
de los yunques benignos
de la hacendosa suerte.

   Vacante
rectitud.
Transitoria, mi carne
finará más aún.

(El Mensajero, p.11)

Tatters:
beacons: dry riverbeds
of the benign anvils
of industrious destiny.

    Empty
rectitude.
Transitory, my flesh
will end even more.

These tattered rags serve as beacons, reminding me of the past and warning me of the ravages of Time. The dry rivers, other beacons, also express Time's destructive power: raging rivers have become dry riverbeds. Fate, industrious and hardworking, brings everything to an end.

With its emptiness, death is the only true state of integrity, that entropic state towards which all life moves and in which all life culminates. The tension and imperfections of life see themselves resolved through its rectitude. Each moment of my life witnesses a movement of disintegration. When I reach the end, my body —even in its lifeless state— will continue that movement of disintegration.

Entretanto el pasado, hacia la nada

Entretanto el pasado, hacia la nada
– constreñir, afligir:
pérfida, la adiaforia, solapada –,
hacia el pasado avanza el porvenir.

(Poesiectomía, p.80)

As the past advances towards nothingness
– to restrict, to afflict:
treacherous, the adiaphoron,* devious – ,
the future advances towards the past.

*Adiaphoron: Greek philosophical term, an action that morality neither endorses nor condemns.

1. Life and Death

Time ceaselessly flows...backwards. Tomorrow becomes today, today becomes yesterday, and yesterday fades into oblivion. Once it is gone, time is never recuperated.

Time restricts and afflicts life with its perpetual movement from future to past. Morally neutral – adiaphoron – it doesn't make any demand. One can use one's time allotted in complete freedom, but its movement, barely perceptible, treacherous, devious, gives the individual the false impression that many years remain, only to suddenly discover that death has arrived.

¿Posteridad?

¿Posteridad?
¿Superávit? ¿Decoro?
¿Ínterin? ¿Otra etapa
de anulación? ¿Reposo?

  La máquina
se desbandó.
Se empalará:
mondongo.

        *
    *   *

      Oh
     tizne,
   te diriges
impersuasiblemente hacia tu No.

(La Opción, p. 20)

Posterity?
Surplus? Decorum?
Interim? Another stage
of annulment? Repose?

The machine
fell apart.
It will stiffen:
tripe.

*
* *

Oh
soot,
you head
obstinately towards your No.

1. Life and Death

What is this state of being commonly known as death?

All that remains behind after I leave? An excess of matter that remains after the disappearance of consciousness? A life beyond my own limited conception of what it means to live? Decorum that relieves those who are still concerned about me? An interim state between my current life and a life still to come? Another stage of annihilation, like the imperceptible deterioration and the inexorable destruction of being that I experience in this life? A state of

rest?

I know that in the moment of death the miraculous machine of my body and consciousness will disperse. The corpse, stiff in rigor mortis: mere remains.

Could there be more? Can consciousness overcome death? One dies: ashes. Yet consciousness endures in the body's smallest element: soot that I award the power to understand. And even this microscopic element of consciousness directs itself obstinately toward its own negation.

In the second and third stanzas, the poet responds to the questions posed in the first. Death may be any of the possibilities mentioned at the poem's beginning. Indisputable, the destruction and transformation of the body. The last stanza's description of the continuation of consciousness, along with its persistent movement toward self-annihilation, reflects universal entropic

processes.

Con su soga oportuna me ahorca

Con su soga oportuna me ahorca
la baldía intemperie de duendes:
estropajo que arrimo de emblema:
ataúd enroscado, azacel.
Una gota de agua me anhela.

Es danzar con la hostil deserción:
el presagio al revés y cumplido.

Por cordura de harapos garduños,
aflojar lo postrero. ¡Es huirme!
Va a caer y mi sino se tensa,
abrevando la fiebre en cenit:
alfiler que se incrusta en la greda.

¡Sí! ¡Permíteme oír cómo cae
esa gota de agua, Dios mío!

(El Zócalo, p. 15)

With its timely rope
the sterile harshness of elves hangs me:
scrubber that I take as an emblem:
coiled coffin, scapegoat.
A drop of water yearns for me.

   It's to dance with the hostile desertion:
the portent reversed and fulfilled.

   Through the wisdom of cutpurse rags,
to let go of the last one. It's to flee from myself!
It's going to fall and my fate tenses,
slaking the fever at its zenith:
a pin that embeds itself in the clay.

   Yes! Let me hear how
that drop of water falls, my God!

Only too willingly do I sacrifice my life to the sterile harshness of irrationality and erotic desire. I rapidly flee life. The emblems of this attitude are many: a scouring pad, to wipe away the grime of my existence; a coffin; the evasion of reality that the scapegoat symbolizes. In the midst of my plunge towards death, life –a humble drop of water – seeks me.

This movement of mine towards death: what is it? I rejoice in the desertion of myself, the most hostile act imaginable. And my future? Since I neither desire nor accept change, the prediction of my future is already fulfilled: it can only be the same as my past.

Change is possible. Through the wisdom of the pickpocket's rags, those tattered remnants of clothing that represent a free and unconventional life, I abandon all that I previously held dear. The drop of water is about to fall and my own destiny tenses as I merge with it. Slaking the fire in its trajectory, the drop of water becomes consumed as it accomplishes its life's work.

Yes! I must live my own life! God, let me once again hear and understand the fall of that humble drop of water! I want to be with myself during every minute up to death: to inform myself of the fall of the drop of water that I am until my final moment.

In contrast with the negative images at the beginning of the poem, that insignificant drop of water acts with consciousness and purpose. The speaker's plea invigorates it: reaffirmation!

CHAPTER 2

Knowledge and Self-Knowledge

"Florecí", brilla el pájaro.

2. Knowledge and Self-Knowledge

«Florecí», brilla el pájaro.
La flor brilla: «Volé».
«Estáis equivocados.»
...Por supuesto, los tres.

(Poesiectomía, p. 98)

"I flowered," glows the bird.
The flower glows: "I flew."
"You are both wrong."
...Of course, all three.

2. Knowledge and Self-Knowledge

What is the source of knowledge? How can one know oneself? "Florecí" imagines a conversation between two protagonists with the poet as observer. In doing so, it articulates the depth of the misconceptions that human beings have of themselves.

Thinking that it is a flower, the bird glows with pride; thinking that it is a bird, the flower glows in the same way. One can be blind about oneself even to the point of taking pride in one's own misconception! Without objective information from the external world, the subjective viewpoint is rarely correct.

The observer – the poet – notices his own misconception.

Observing the two and himself, the poet takes an even larger view, noting that both the objective and subjective points of view are incorrect. This observation also implies that both points of view contain true aspects of reality. If the bird and flower are mistaken, then the observer is correct, and if the observer is mistaken, then the bird and the flower have captured reality. Both points of view – the objective and the subjective – simultaneously contain correct and incorrect conceptions.

Knowledge is subjective as well as objective. Subjective impressions may be enormously erroneous. Nor is there certainty that what we understand "objectively" is correct.

> The truth is, always, a challenge.

ACADEMIA

ACADEMIA

¿Bazar: grúa: merced
de cilindros: península:
migala: itinerario
de hiedra: aparador
frondoso? El sanedrín
del pupitre, en la audacia
del tapete: mi aljibe.

(El Mensajero, p. 16)

ACADEMIA

Bazaar: crane: mercy
of cylinders: peninsula:
tarantula: itinerary
of ivy: leafy
sideboard? The sanhedrin
of the desk, in the boldness
of the rug: my cistern.

What is academia?

A marketplace that offers wares from around the world, with varying degrees of quality, from both honest and dishonest vendors? Treasures are there to be found; but the wrong choices, costly.

A crane useful for the construction of the edifice that is my life? The machine, powerful and effective under the control of a trained and experienced operator. Do I have the intelligence and maturity to operate it?

A diploma: the gift mercifully awarded after years of work? The cylinder of the diploma is empty, the diploma only a piece of paper. Is this symbol, so important in the external world, more important to me than what I have learned?

A community marginally connected to the mainland of society, but with its own separate existence? Does this peninsular world form the totality of my world?

A creature that spins webs to permeate, trap, and devour all aspects of my being?

A voyage that lasts many years, without a fixed destination? Even after I arrive, is my final destination the place where I really wanted to go?

A venue reserved for the privileged, where I become knowledgeable, cultured, a member of the elite? A ferocious competition where the law of the jungle prevails? Or, perhaps, that same jungle, hidden beneath the veneer of culture and privilege?

Academia: in effect, all of the above. Examination results, grades and diplomas constitute the judgment of the institution and my own self-judgment. True academia: the judgment of knowledge itself, knowledge that wants to be understood, that demands time at the desk, effort, and objectivity. This, the only judgment that really matters.

And the other part of academia? The expression of knowledge, for what is knowledge worth without its expression? That expression demands boldness from me, for true knowledge often contradicts current thinking. To work, to learn, and to express up to the limit of my ability: the ballast that stabilizes my life and thought: the cistern that refreshes and nourishes me.

Singular cuchitril:

Singular cuchitril:
cortinaje: te manchas,
te empelusas,

te desgastas,
te arrugas.
¿Te aludo a ti o a mí?

(La Opción, p. 82)

Singular hovel:
curtains: you become stained,
you cover yourself with fuzz,

you wear out,
you become wrinkled.
Do I allude to you or to me?

2. Knowledge and Self-Knowledge

You are a hovel. Unique? Yes, a small and cluttered house that you fill with trash. Its drawn curtains shut out your light of your true being. You become stained with inessential activities and thoughts, you settle for a superficial life, you wear out mind and body in perpetual attempts to avoid your true self. In this way, you wrinkle and approach the end.

Do these critiques apply to me as well as to you? Am I alluding to myself when I speak to you? More than anyone, I know how I tarnish myself with useless thoughts and unnecessary actions, how I cover myself with superficialities, how I age without living my real life. Suddenly, criticizing you, I have awakened.

To criticize another is easy. Do I have the courage and will to examine, with objectivity and sincerity, my own being? The last word of the poem's first line and the last word of its last line are connected through both assonant rhyme and accentuation. The poet uses rhyme to connect the "cuchitril" (hovel) with the personal pronoun "mí" (me), suggesting that the "hovel" is the speaker himself.

ADMISERICÓRDIAM

ADMISERICÓRDIAM

Una lechuza, inquieta, en un altar,
solfea Euclides, Dargüin y Volter:
«¿He de aburrirme para descansar?
Sorber. Tragar.
Sorber.»

Y Dios, en sus abismos,
con ombligo.

(Auge, p. 63)

ADMISERICORDIAM

An owl, anxious, on an altar,
sol-fas Euclid, Darwin and Voltaire:
"Must I bore myself in order to rest?
To sip. To swallow.
To sip."

And God, in his abysses,
with his navel.

2. Knowledge and Self-Knowledge

The title: Spanish version of a Latin word: plea for compassion that the poet reveals for humanity and God. This poem addresses the attitude, methods, and objective of learning, using the owl as a symbol of humanity to avoid condemning the human being directly.

An owl: innocent being who, religiously, hoping for rest, wants to know. It studies the mathematics of Euclid, the biology of Darwin, and the philosophy of Voltaire. The more it learns, the more it knows that it doesn't know. "Is my goal to become bored, so that I will be able to rest?"

The owl discovers that its learning methods are ineffective. "Can I learn mathematics, biology and philosophy by singing scales? I sip, swallow and sip them more and more."

On the altar of learning and with the desire to know, the owl, with an imperfect method, approaches divinity.

God in his abysses, without studying nor learning, contemplates his navel.

*

* *

Euclid, Darwin, and Voltaire: generous and intelligent men, but far from the truth.

Religion: glorification of an unknown entity.

And true knowledge? After the disappearance of "our" planet?

ADMISERICORDIAM!

SABIDURÍA

SABIDURÍA

Expresar la evidencia
con palabras,
con números,
con silencio y sonido,
con colores:

trasmitir,
proteger
con cabriolas, con gestos,
para así regalarme: regalar
defensas nutritivas

al ser del ser, tan poderoso y tenue.

(Trébol de Nueve, p.7)

WISDOM

To express the evidence
with words,
with numbers,
with silence and sound,
with colors:

to transmit,
to protect
with capers, with gestures,
to give myself a gift in this way: to give
nutritious defenses

to the being of being, so powerful and so weak.

What is wisdom?

To fully understand the evidence and use all possible resources to transmit that information. More than the understanding of an idea, wisdom is also expression and communication. The goal? Full understanding, by means of channels of communication, movement, gestures, tone.

The goal of wisdom? To provide nutrition to defend one's real being. Weak, it demands nutrition to defend itself from social norms and biological imperatives.

This: the gift that I must give myself.

Derroté mis efigies:

Derroté mis efigies:
pestañearon – tamiz –:
los corceles de límites
resollaron – ardid –:
murallas de furor sobre mis torreones.

(El Zócalo, p. 11)

I defeated my effigies:
they blinked – a sieve:
the steeds of limits
panted – a ruse:
walls of fury over my great towers.

Within me exists a multitude of identities: those that other people think I am, and mine. I can, in public, play different roles, but for myself, one. Did I use my intelligence to resolve problems, or did I allow my emotions to rule? I conquered my prior beliefs: my false representations of who I was. Reflecting, I came to understand them and fought steadfastly to defeat them. Facing my resolve, although strong and resisting, their defenses were porous. This porosity was their strength: I believed that I had defeated them, but they still existed, intact.

The "steeds of limits" – my strong and beautiful beliefs, false and limited versions of myself – another ruse. They were not exhausted: they were waiting to again impose their will.

Defeated for now, these enemy identities of the fortified towers of my true self. With all their deceptive and attractive representations, their porosity and their ruses, they failed. Impotent for the moment, they raised a deafening howl against my defenses: the great strength that unifies me to my authentic self.

"*Con mutabilidad*

«Con mutabilidad
meteórica absorber
rozagantes querubes:
leve domestiquez

– fundamental
costumbre –,
fingida realidad.
Descubramos

la nueva calavera:
frustración."
Y el sabio, sabio,

para pensar
mejor,
se sacó

la cabeza.

(Oó, o, p. 77)

"With meteoric
mutability to absorb
blooming cherubs:
light tameness

– fundamental
custom – ,
feigned reality.
Let us discover

the new skull:
frustration."
And the sage,

in order to think
better,
pulled out

his head.

2. Knowledge and Self-Knowledge

The sage spoke:

"We are born with the propensity for change, and over time develop that talent, to be able to mutate with the rapidity of a meteor. We possess a frivolous meekness that allows us to absorb new versions of reality, fully embracing each successive version as the real truth.

Let's discover the new skull: frustration can help us to understand that all these ephemeral realities are false and that the reality of our existence lies on the other side."

The sage openly extracted his thoughts from the society in which he lived,

to think and understand better.

Volubles alternativas

Volubles alternativas
germinan – germinarán –
perversidades hermosas.
En andrajos, la bondad.

¿Las premuras de la insidia
germinan? ¡Germinarán!
Cuántos aromas, la aurora...
Ni un bocado, por bondad.

Acumulo melodías
– germinan (¿germinarán?) –
sobre el atril de la escoria.
Lo sostengo con bondad.

(Poesiectomía, p. 95)

Voluble alternatives
germinate – will germinate –
beautiful perversities.
In tatters, kindness.

    Do the urgencies of treachery
germinate? They will!
How many aromas, the dawn…
Not a bite, through kindness.

    I accumulate melodies
– they germinate (will they?) –
on the lectern of dross.
I support it with kindness.

Lies have engendered perversities in the past and present. They will continue doing so in the future. These perversities appear beautiful, since lies at times are more beautiful than the truth. They are voluble because they must convince. The truth is silent: it simply exists. Its kindness: in tatters, due to the lack of attention that the world offers it.

The opposite of thoughtfulness and care: urgency, treachery, self-betrayal. Will haste, with the lack of attention that accompanies it, continue engendering even more treachery?

The dawn of each day brings only the weakest positive possibilities.

I, at least, accumulate melodies – a kind sweetness – against the dross of the world.

CHAPTER 3

God and Nature

No el cadáver de Dios lo que medito

No el cadáver de Dios lo que medito,
ni su traslumbramiento lo que muerdo:
venero de veneros cuanto agito
    y gano y beso y pierdo.

A dentelladas, esplendor de ala
total en mi espadaña azul, resiste.
Copa, satisfaciéndome, resbala.
    Pedernal fibra, embiste.

Oh campana de túnicas divinas:
    linfas siempre divinas
    en las cumbres divinas...

(El Zócalo, p. 33)

It is neither the corpse of God that I contemplate,
nor his radiance that I bite;
origin of origins as I agitate
      and win and kiss and lose.

With tooth and nail, splendor of total wing
in my blue steeple, resist.
Cup, satisfying me, slip.
      Flint fiber, attack.

Oh bell of robes divine:
      lymphs always divine
      in the heights divine…

This poem is found in the first book of the tetralogy *Cortejo y Epinicio*, the human being in his first years.

God is dead. I neither meditate on His cadaver nor does His radiance illuminate me. Instead, I embrace the experiences that life offers, positive and negative, and find my own Creator.

To my splendor – my consciousness, my essence, - I order: resist temptations! To the cup that satisfies: slip from my grasp! To my strength – rigor of my own moral fiber - I insist: charge, attack! Consciousness, will, and action: key ingredients for my auto-creation.

My being is clothed in the divinity of the mind and that of the body, to achieve its highest potential. The lymph is divine, since it sustains the functions that keep body and brain alive. Human consciousness is also divine; the collaboration of consciousness with the body permits the human being to attain his highest potential.

Varias malezas:

Varias malezas:
efetá
de harapos.
– ¿Enjundia la conciencia?
– ¿Por qué me lo preguntas, Jeová?
– ¿Prohibido preguntártelo?

(Oó, o, p. 73)

Various weeds:
obstinacy
of rags.
– What is the reason for consciousness?
– Why do you ask me that, Jehovah?
– Is it forbidden to ask you that?

Unlike a beautifully manicured lawn, my clothes: rags. I act consciously. Is consciousness a fundamental element?

*

* *

The universe that God created demonstrates the lack of consciousness: expansions, contractions, births, deaths, multiplicities of random occurrences with good and evil intermingled. God wants to know if the human being uses consciousness, at times or always.

*

* *

The poem manifests the limited employment of consciousness in the cosmos and, of course, in human conduct.

TAJRIJIM

TAJRIJIM

Honrando lo impoluto de un laudable mefisto
sobre este basural de eficacia omitida,
la prole de Ramrram y la prole de Cristo
veneran la juiciosa culebra parricida.

Letame de tarántulas, hemisferio de flema,
lápida de las lápidas: reclamo mi sudario
        Cloaca, tu diadema:
           ¡mi sudario!

...Negligencia, me acoges,
sin indagar con larvas, en tus trojes.

                (El Mensajero, p. 101).

TAJRIJIM

Honoring the purity of a laudable mephistopheles
on this trash heap of omitted efficacy,
the progeny of Ramrram and the progeny of Christ
venerate the judicious snake parricide.

Fertilizer of tarantulas, hemisphere of phlegm,
tombstone of tombstones: I reclaim my shroud.
Sewer, your diadem:
my shroud!

...Negligence, you welcome me,
without investigating with larvae, in your granaries.

The name that the Jewish religion gives to white burial shrouds.

TAJRIJIM

In contrast with the belief in God and an everlasting life, humanity, judiciously, honors the objective and scientific view of the ugly, inefficient, and worthless world in which we live. With humanity's eyes open to secular knowledge and, in consequence, God's figurative death, we live our lives, not His; the world is ours, not His; and true understanding becomes possible.

With eyes now open I see the world as the mountain of rubbish that it is: dung of tarantulas, hemisphere of phlegm, tombstone of tombstones and inevitable death. My burial shrouds? Not the *tajrijim* but the earth. And the diadem of the sewer? The human and animal remains that transform inert matter into new life.

Unconscious, the earth of the Earth doesn't reflect. It simply accepts.

Cuando, de vez en noche, soy real,

Cuando, de vez en noche, soy real,
sobre el teclado azul de mi estandarte
aúlla el horizonte, vertical.
Piano del mundo, déjame afinarte.

(Auge, p. 7)

When, sometimes at night, I am real,
over the blue keyboard of my standard
howls the horizon, vertical.
Piano of the world, let me tune you.

At times, in the night, I am authentically real. I capture in my celestial keyboard – my standard: my mind – the desperate score of an erroneous horizon.

In the moments when I am truly real, I listen: World, you howl. Your horizon is not horizontal, but vertical; the reality that I achieve exposes the lie of your appearance. Like a human being with anguish or despair when his nature becomes visible, you howl when I show you your truth.

World, let the celestial keyboard of my consciousness tune – put in order

– your piano.

DEPEAPÁ

DEPEAPÁ

Sosa,
la novelita
rosa
del falso firmamento.

Cuando la terminé
me percaté
de que nunca fue escrita,
no porque no aferrara algún talento.
Por axiomática. ¡Por infinita!

(El Mensajero, p. 120)

FROM BEGINNING TO END

Bland,
the romance
novelette
of the false firmament.

When I finished it
I realized
that it was never written,
not because it didn't contain some talent.
Because it is axiomatic. Because it is infinite!

3. God and Nature

Our current understanding of the multiverse is a romance novel: unfortunately, imprecise. Time and space are only two elements of "our" universe. What existed before? To read or write a book without beginning or end?

This narrative has for authors the most cultivated and intelligent intellectuals of each era.

Can one, in a finite container, capture infinity?

CHAPTER 4

Development and Regression

NATURALEZA MUERTA

NATURALEZA MUERTA

Porvenir:
¿moscas?
    Vaivén:
rincón de cuna: alfil
con una sien.

(Oó, o, p. 89)

STILL LIFE

Future:
flies?
Going and coming:
corner of a cradle: bishop
with a brain.

Nature is constantly bringing along death.

What is the portrait of my existence? A voyage to end up as food for the flies of death, since I am a "natural" fragment.

But also, I have come to attain my being: to occupy a corner of that brief vital cradle.

Unlike the bishop on the chessboard, I have a brain.

The first word of the poem – future – contains the word "to come": to come to my person, to come to my life.

The rhyme – come and temple – expresses: use your brain!: approach yourself, your fleeting nature that is both alive and friend! At least defend yourself from inevitable death, through a coming and going that protects your reason for being.

Ricos

4. Development and Regression

Ricos
yermos:
atletas esfumados.
El mapa de mis sueños

aloja más espacio que el espacio.
¿Te entulleces?
¡Unidos,
guiñándonos,

crucemos!:
puentes
– los multiversos –
necios, ínfimos.

(Auge, p. 231)

Rich
badlands:
vanished athletes.
The map of my dreams

accommodates more space than space.
Do you cripple yourself?
United,
winking at each other,

let's cross!:
bridges
– the multiverses –
idiotic, tiny.

The riches of the badlands of my interior world – parts of my being that worked with discipline and attention – have disappeared.

My dreams: infinite. You, my dreamer, do you obstruct yourself, detain yourself, cripple yourself?

We are two: one, asleep, and the other, capable, without direction.

Let's cross, together, the enormous insignificance of reality.

All, in comparison with my dreams, foolish and tiny.

... e interrogar a Dios, al techo, al adoquín,

...e interrogar a Dios, al techo, al adoquín,
al vanidoso círculo ovalado,
para aferrar la sensatez del rayo:
        sucedí.

(Poesiectomía, p.82)

. . . and to question God, the roof, the cobblestone,
the conceited oval circle,
in order to grasp the wisdom of the ray:
        I occurred.

The initial ellipsis indicates that the poem is a fragment of an urgent investigation.

I was born; I occurred; I am alive.

Possibly I am here to ask questions. Why God? Why a roof over me? Why the sky over the roof? Why the cobblestones below me, and earth below the cobblestones? What are these natural constructions or these made by man? What is the reason for my mental creations? And that of my existence?

My struggle to find answers: essential.

Mi calavera, huérfana,

Mi calavera, huérfana,
desde su inoperancia sin asueto,
me confronta: "Sé avaro:
cultiva, en la trastienda,
los tamaños correctos,
el la subtrés, el blanco sobre el blanco."

(Poesiectomía, p. 29)

My skull, an orphan,
from its ineffectiveness,
confronts me: "Be stingy:
cultivate, in the back room,
the correct sizes,
the concert pitch, the bullseye over the bullseye."

A dry bone without a future, my skull – a counselor in a state of eternal uselessness – confronts me from its present: "Don't give anything away, be correct with yourself – in perfect harmony – so that your orchestra – your being – will be in condition to play perfectly: to reach the goal beyond the goal: to live your life with absolute plenitude: invisible treasure of the visible treasure."

LA PRESTÍSIMA

LA PRESTÍSIMA

Mi favorita bisnieta
se casó
consigo misma.
Invitó a la recepción
a su familia:

a su giba, a su jardín,
a su quiltro, a su vainilla,
a su montón
de tarea
y a su yerma lozanía.

(La Noche Antes, p. 22)

THE QUICKEST

My favorite great-granddaughter
married
herself.
She invited to the reception
her family:

her hump, her garden,
her mutt, her vanilla,
her mountain
of work
and her barren vigor.

The irony of the title shows that even old age is a brief occurrence: a great rapidity is the witness of another great rapidity.

How, at any age, to try to be happy.

MANANTIAL

MANANTIAL

¿Quién
al alba de la tarde?
¿Yo: tu imagen?
Dolías en el llano de las cosas que rompen.

   El agua, entre las aguas,
horadaba,
subía. ¿Tú? Crecíamos
hacia el prodigio
del
encuentro.

   Cortamos los racimos:
imagen contra imagen:
rebeliones.

(Trébol de Nueve, p.45)

WELLSPRING

Who
at the dawn of the evening?
I: your image?
You were hurting in the plain of things that
break.

    The water, between the waters,
pierced through,
rose. You? We were growing
towards the miracle
of the
encounter.

    We cut the clusters:
image against image:
rebellions.

An earlier version of this poem was published in *La Enredadera del Júbilo* in 1952.
 The joy of our most contented friendship confronted our consciousnesses.
 The water of the miraculous wellspring pierced us.
 Were we, you and I, one?
 Were we only moving to a marvelous meeting?
 Both images: only rebellions.

YEMA

4. Development and Regression

YEMA

«¡Que, civilizador,
el error
hable!"
La oferta, soslayable.

(Auge, p. 95)

YOLK

"**L**et
the error
speak, civilizer!"
The offer, avoidable.

What, undoubtedly, produces progress?

The experience of error – its recognition – enables one to escape from the embryonic state.

Through error, we develop, civilize ourselves and mature.

Error is the yolk of the human species.

Will we use it?

CHAPTER 5

Eroticism

Gesto, dique, tarugo,

Gesto, dique, tarugo,
miriñaque de estío,
placenta de sigilo,
peripecia: concúbito.

(Poesiectomía, p. 15)

Gesture, dike, plug,
crinoline of summer,
placenta of silence,
vicissitude: copulation.

An example of Rosenmann-Taub's succinct poetic style, this eleven-word poem contains six different representations of sexual intercourse.

Copulation: gesture. Physical attraction? Love? Desire? Power? Ego? Understanding?

Copulation: a dike against death, loneliness, time... Affectionate liberation from the external world.

Copulation: a plug that guards corporal communication.

Copulation: a summer crinoline, a pretense of splendor and well-being.

Copulation: a placenta of silence that nourishes silence and isolation.

Copulation: a vicissitude, an incident, a casual adventure.

MADRIGAL

MADRIGAL

Te dije: «Bálsamo del multiverso.»
Te dije: "Enselva y sacia tus espigas."
Te dije: "Breña y litoral y cítara."
Con mi silencio te diré: "Rodemos."

(El Zócalo, p. 123)

MADRIGAL

I said to you: "Balm of the multiverse."
I said to you: "Scatter your wheat ears in the forest
                                              and sate them."
I said to you: "Brushwood and seacoast and zither."
With my silence I will say to you: "Let's roll together."

5. Eroticism

From the chapter "En las lavas sensuales" of *El* Zócalo, the first volume of the tetralogy *Cortejo y Epinicio*. An immaculate idealistic vision of the erotic experience.

The poet speaks to his lover, addressing the central concerns of their lives.

You are the balm that salves wounds and eases pain. Even more: balm that extends through all.

Allow your internal kernels to extend themselves and become satiated.

Compare your beauty to that of plants, the beach and music.

In silence: "Let us embrace."

CONTRAESPEJOS

CONTRAESPEJOS

(**F**ortuitas colgaduras.)
...Bujía, ciñes siglos,
sometiéndote: inculcas
disfraz en el jergón arrepentido.

Fatigas sórdidas
se nutren. Hueros,
los tobillos sollozan.
(¿Multiplicar? ¡Cubiertos!)

(El Mensajero, p. 21)

AGAINSTMIRRORS

    (**F**ortuitous hangings.)
...Candle, you restrict centuries,
yielding: you imprint a disguise on the repentant mattress.

    Sordid hardships
nourish themselves. Worthless,
the ankles sob.
(Multiply? Covers!)

Mirrors abound in the bedroom; fortunately, they are covered by curtains, so neither my lover nor I can see each other. The room, illuminated only by soft and flickering candlelight, sheds our years. As we yield to nature's program of reproduction, the candle imprints a disguise on the mattress where we copulate. You yield easily. The mattress is ashamed, repentant for its obedience to that task.

With procreation, those sordid hardships of which life consists continue nourishing themselves. The ankles, left to their own devices, suffer. Unfortunately, they are under the control of their unconscious master; they sob at their predicament.

To procreate? Desire hides. Tiredness grows: dominates the bodies: prevents new life: "I don't want to marry you because I desire you and because I yearn for children."

En las lavas sensuales busco siempre el regreso

En las lavas sensuales busco siempre el regreso
a los cielos profundos del río maternal.
Promontorio de cuervos, andábata leal,
volver anhelo al vientre por oasis de hueso.

(El Zócalo, p. 130)

In the sensual lavas, I always search for the return
to the profound heavens of the maternal river.
Promontory of crows, loyal blindfolded gladiator,
I long to return to the womb through the oasis of bone.

5. Eroticism

I pursue, through copulation, my mother's womb.

I – mountain of help,

persevering blind gladiator* –

came from there surrounded and nourished by its osseous amniotic paradise.

---

*Gladiator who wore a helmet with a closed visor, i.e., fought blindfolded.

Me imito:

5. Eroticism

Me imito:
blasfemables
acrobacias:
vorágines:
vestigio
de biznagas.

(La Noche Antes, p. 90)

I imitate myself:
blasphemous
acrobatics:
maelstroms:
vestige
of cacti.

5. Eroticism

From *La Noche Antes*, the fourth volume of the tetralogy *Cortejo y Epinicio*: the last period of life of the human being. The poem addresses the erotic experience during this period.

I have my own understanding of the erotic experience. Developed during my adolescence, it remains constant. However, I blaspheme maelstroms of doubt and confusion. Why do I continue imitating myself? What prevents me from adapting myself to my internal changes?

The cacti resisted. Now I understand the fruitlessness of my habits, thoughts and suppositions.

>Do I have the will and strength to accept to change?

CHAPTER 6

Family, Friends, and Others

Tu estricto cúmulo

Tu estricto cúmulo
se abasteció:
servirte, por servirme:
colmándome, colmarte:

   perplejidad
ardiente:
rifirrafe:
sumisión:

   aprendiéndote,
servirme, por servirte:
colmándote, colmarme.

   No la unidad
de dos,
sino, invencible, la unidad de uno.

(La Opción, p. 212)

Your strict accumulation
was provided:
to serve yourself, by serving me:
fulfilling me, to fulfill yourself:

   burning
perplexity:
a squabble:
submission:

   learning from yourself,
to serve me, by serving yourself:
fulfilling yourself, to fulfill me.

   Not the unity
of two,
but, invincible, the unity of one.

6. Family, Friends and Others 155

This poem belongs to "Oasis," from the third volume – *La Opción* – of *Cortejo y Epinicio*.

During the course of your life, you accumulated experiences and habits that were neither casual nor arbitrary. You served me by serving yourself, you fulfilled me by fulfilling yourself.

Through dialogues, squabbles and submissions, we attained the invincible unity.

¡Vastedad de lo

¡Vastedad de lo
obvio!
Tú:
yo:
nosotros:
cuán insólito azul.

(La Noche Antes, p. 145)

Vastness of the
obvious!
You:
I:
we:
what extraordinary blue.

This poem belongs to "Oasis," from *La Noche Antes*. It celebrates the miracle of friendship.

Daily experience shapes my understanding of the world, the other, and myself. With the accumulation of these daily experiences over the course of many years, my understanding now seems obvious. I become blind to its true significance; the vast becomes trivial, and what I consider trivial, vast.

My experience of you, seemingly so known, obvious. Is it really possible to know another human being? The obvious is, in reality, a miracle.

My experience of myself: the same. I well know my tendencies and habits, my ways of thinking and acting. I take all this, so obvious, for granted. Yet to be alive, to be conscious, to know oneself, is that not also a miracle?

More important than any individual alone, is *we*: the two of us in relationship. Mutual trust: an incomparable pearl: amazingly celestial.

La genilla de tu mampara

La genilla de tu mampara
me condujo.
Las espirales de tus muros
me excitaron.
Tu premeditada
pomposidad: taladro.

(La Noche Antes, p. 89)

The pupil of your inner door
led me.
The spirals of your walls
excited me.
Your premeditated
pompousness: a drill.

The poem comes from "En las lavas sensuales" of *La Noche Antes*.

An old man is affected at almost seeing a female body. The difficulty arouses him.

What he is unable to see rejuvenates him: it drills through time.

OLIGOPSONIO

OLIGOPSONIO

Ultrabaratos,
ultrabaratísimos,
a domicilio,
frascos
para guardar
honestidad.

(La Opción, p. 107)

OLIGOPSONY

Ultracheap
superultracheap,
door to door,
bottles in which
to store
honesty.

To sell bottles of honesty? Who wants to buy them? Oligopsony, useless.

Dishonesty is a good business.

¡Ir, sin reclamos,

¡Ir, sin reclamos,
por cordial atajo!
Cálida, el hada: "¿Vamos?"
«¿Adónde?» Helada, el hada se contrajo.

(Auge, p. 75)

To go, without complaints,
by way of a friendly shortcut!
The fairy, warmly: "Shall we go?"
"Where?" Frozen, the fairy contracted.

6. Family, Friends and Others

An opportunity arises that can rapidly take me to an unknown destination. The opportunity attracts, but also poses questions and risks. Do I trust in fate and blindly forge ahead, with neither precaution nor questions? Or do I proceed slowly, seeking information to assess potential risks and rewards?

As a child, I unhesitatingly leaped at these opportunities, knowing that my good fairy would not steer me wrong. Now, an adult, more prudent. As a consequence, the majority of times the opportunity disappears; my generous good fairy demands a trust which I am unwilling to give.

To leap or to hesitate when opportunity knocks at the door: which of these postures is correct? Both...and neither. I want to experience life to the fullest and to protect myself from unknown dangers. How to do both?

CHAPTER 7

Consciousness and Unconsciousness

FÍSICO

FÍSICO

Polea de celajes:
hacia las medianoches del guarro amanecer,
    los incas y sus pajes.

Trompo encarnado – predilecta muerte -,
giras para aprender a no moverte
    y desaparecer.

¿Quizá de lo tortuoso unas señales?
¿Hubo entre estas instancias pensamiento?
    Calvarios: por pañales.
    ¡Égida de escarmiento!

(El Mensajero, p.28)

PHYSICAL

Pulley of cloudscapes:
from the filthy sunrise towards the midnights,
the incas and their pages.

Incarnate top – preferred death – ,
you spin to learn to not move
and to disappear.

Perhaps some signs of the tortuous?
Was there thought amidst these instances?
Calvaries: for diapers.
Shield of punishment!

Life: an unstoppable movement through time that begins with a painful and bloody birth and continues up to the midnight of death. This movement is as mechanical and inexorable as the movement of clouds dragged by a celestial pulley. This movement dominates everything. Life: a series of cloudscapes that eternally obscure one's own reality and destiny.

Irrelevant if you are the king or his servant.

You: a top that spins to learn what is immobile. Through this constant movement you disappear – your preferred death – not only from others but from yourself.

Did you notice any signs of this torture? Starting from birth, you bartered death for life – calvaries for diapers – preferring the lesser punishment of unconsciousness as your shield against the struggle of a conscious life that constitutes the greater punishment.

The poem establishes a parallel between the inflexible laws of nature and those of the human sphere that engender the conscious and unconscious life of the human being.

EREMITA

EREMITA

Ruina farándula, mi biografía:
majestuosa tristeza
con torpe galería:
«Retractándome, avanzo.»

Vulneré la belleza
de un casto perigonio.
Mi extensa soltería:
quilométricas piezas sin descanso.

Mi ovante matrimonio:
los interludios de ilusiva pieza:
¿futuro que ocurrió?

Mi delirio bosteza:
– Tu yo
te obedeció.

(Oó, o, p.101)

HERMIT

A theater world in ruins, my biography:
majestic sadness
with a thick-witted gallery:
"Retracting, I advance."

I damaged the beauty
of a chaste perigon.
My lengthy bachelorhood:
nonstop kilometric plays.

My triumphant marriage:
the intermissions of an illusory play:
a future that happened?

My delirium yawns:
– Your I
obeyed you.

With its title that invokes solitude and alienation as its point of departure, this poem presents a chilling portrait of directionless life.

The story of my life: a long and varied series of plays that for one reason or another, failed. How late do I recognize the triviality of my life in comparison with its original potential! I recognize, for the first time, the possibilities that opened up to me, and this sadness is my first experience that corresponds to the royal nature of my being. I share that emotion with my "thick-witted audience": that idiotic part of myself that ties me to external objectives. I perceive, in this theater in ruins, that my failures propelled me forward: they were, in spite of their negative appearance, my true successes.

At the moment of conception, the seed from which I emerged was pure, perfect, unique, and beautiful. Nevertheless, starting from that moment, I damaged it. Instead of joining in matrimony with my true being I remained a bachelor, acting the roles of others in thousands of productions without respite.

Then, an epiphany: I achieved a triumphal understanding and union with my real being: I married myself. Unfortunately, there was no happy ending; my failures, negativity, self-deception, and laziness continued. My epiphany turned out to be nothing more than a short intermission in those endless illusory plays that constitute my life. Was this marriage a fraud? Has my future, before appearing, become my past?

Bored with their never-ending influence in my life, my confusions, complaints, and consternations yawn in front of me: "You obeyed only yourself." I don't want to hear them. Yet it was I who chose the roles, directed the play; it was I at rehearsals, I who acted, I the audience and the theater.

On the surface my life has been full and vibrant. In reality, alienated from my essence, that of a hermit. The theater, in ruins. And the time? Expired.

Cenit, imploras nadir.

Cenit, imploras nadir.
Talento de sinsentido,
para vivir has vivido.
Morirás para morir.

(Poesiectomía, p. 22)

Zenith, you beg for the nadir.
Talent of nonsense,
in order to live you have lived.
You will die in order to die.

7. Consciousness and Unconsciousness

Poesiectomía: neologism – a surgical operation – created by the poet, to express the truth with exactitude.

Zenith of consciousness and development that begs for nadir – its opposite: – your non-sense pursues meaning, even though it appears in order to disappear.

The capacity for reflection, through unlimited development, provides the capacity to extirpate the oblivion and blindness in which we live.

You will die in order to know secret of the meaning of death.

To live, to die: stages of something more.

Vértigo:

Vértigo:
me sanciono:
gigantez entre intrépidos terrores:
baturrillo.

  ¿Cavilo
desde dónde?
Dependo
−caudaloso

    prisionero
con testigo −
de un efecto

   que malmalicio
mío,
pues, desgraciadamente, soy un hombre.

(Auge, p. 55)

Vertigo:
I punish myself:
immensity between intrepid terrors:
hodgepodge.

   From where
do I reflect?
I rely
– wealthy

   prisoner
with witness –
on an effect

   that I mis-suspect
is mine
since, unfortunately, I am a man.

7. Consciousness and Unconsciousness

I achieve consciousness, but experience it as vertigo. Despite my immensity, audacious terrors inhibit my thoughts and actions. My consciousness produces only a hodgepodge: a disorganized mixture of thoughts and feelings, talents and stupidities.

Where is my center? From what base do I organize myself? I find myself a prisoner. I cannot plead ignorance; I possess an internal witness who knows my capacities and the hodgepodge that I introduce into myself.

The effect of this vertigo: terrors due to an incorrect self-conception, since I am a human being.

*
* *

The individual misinterprets his authentic capacity.

When is the human being human?

Rarely.

Endriago encabritado:

Endriago encabritado:
gladiador:
derrotado
monitor
de albedrío,
talvez, mío.
Caoba nigromante.
Tumba errante.

(El Mensajero, 57)

Rearing monster:
gladiator:
vanquished
monitor
of will,
perhaps, mine.
Mahogany necromancer.
Wandering grave.

This poem of eight lines consists of five complex and interrelated metaphors.
  What am I?
  1: Not by my will, from head to feet, a semi-human monster.
  2: Gladiator who fights due to the will of others.
  3. Imprecise detector that I suppose is mine and which must fail.
  4. Magical tree that divines the future.
  5. Vagabond tomb.

        I am an alien will.

    Perhaps a fighter defeated by death: a wandering tomb

Por un resquicio exiguo

7. Consciousness and Unconsciousness

Por un resquicio exiguo
se ha colado la risa:
desconocida herrumbre,
pelaje de cosquilla:
    mi primera
carcajada en la tierra,
con más fiera agonía,
de fiera pesadumbre,
que mi primer vagido.

(La Noche Antes, p. 18)

Through a trifling opening
has slipped the laugh:
unknown rust,
tickling fur:
      my first
guffaw on earth,
with more ferocious agony,
of ferocious grief,
than my first cry.

The poem describes the initial evident manifestation of consciousness and the tragic nature of the human condition.

The laugh – unknown rust – emerges through the small birth canal and makes itself mine: with its fur it tickles me and provokes my first laugh: a fierce agony, more painful than my first cry.

My laugh? A devastating guffaw: manifestation of consciousness? Reality mocks my transitory appearance.

En el náufrago día de mi nave más bella

7. Consciousness and Unconsciousness

En el náufrago día de mi nave más bella
me encaramé sobre su mastelero
    para mirar el mar.

No había mar: no había ni su huella:
no había ni el vacío de ese día postrero.
    Sólo había mirar.

Miré el mirar del navegar que espero.

(Auge, p. 235)

On the shipwreck day of my most beautiful ship
I climbed its highest mast
> to look at the sea.

There was no sea: there was not even a trace of it:
there was not even the void of that last day.
> There was only looking.

I looked at the looking of the sailing that I await.

In the moment of my death, I decided to look.

Everything had disappeared.

Only the capacity to look remained.

My lucidity looked at that which awaits me.

www.ingramcontent.com/pod-product-compliance
Lightning Source LLC
Chambersburg PA
CBHW021841220426
43663CB00005B/357